THE INNOVATIVE PRAYER LEADER

BY C. TERRELL WHEAT

Practical Strategies for Creating a Life-Changing Prayer Culture in Your Ministry

The Innovative Prayer Leader

Practical Strategies for Creating a Life-Changing Prayer Culture in Your Ministry

Unless otherwise indicated, all scriptural quotations are taken from the Amplified Version of the Holy Bible.

Copyright ©2020 C. Terrell Wheat
P.O Box 2327
Matteson, Illinois 60443
www.cterrellwheat.com
E-mail: info@cterrellwheat.com

All rights reserved. This book or any portion thereof may not be reproduced or used in any manner whatsoever without the express written permission of the publisher except for the use of brief quotation in a book review.

Printed in the United States of America

ISBN - 9798671437041

Gratitude

To the wife of my youth, Tanesha, you have been by my side for nearly half of my life. You are smart, beautiful, wise, loving, caring, and simply amazing! You are the picture of dedication and the ultimate support system. You are the greatest gift that God has given me and I thank God for you. I dedicate this book to you.

To my five sons, Xavier, Courtland, Cameron, Christian, and Caleb, you were my ultimate motivation to finish this book. As a father, one of the lessons that I set out to teach you was, with hard work and God's help, all of your dreams can become reality. This is my first book and I dedicate this book to you.

To the first man who ever believed in me, my father in the ministry, Pastor Harvey Carey, you saw something in me that I did not see in myself. You poured in me and loved me when I was broken. You led me to Christ and discipled me. I shared my dream of being a man of prayer and you did everything in your power to prepare me for that role. I love you and I dedicate this book to you.

To my pastor, John F. Hannah, you are the ultimate model of a man of integrity and a man of prayer. For over a decade you have allowed me to share a platform with you and lead millions in prayer. You have taught me so many things over the years, but three lessons stand out: You taught me how to put my family first, you taught me how to be consistent in the things of God, and you taught me the value of taking the long route. I would not be who I am without you. I dedicate this book to you.

To my best friend in the world, Pastor Shaun Marshall, I pulled you out of the crowd when we were teenagers and encouraged you to get into ministry. You were a diamond in the rough and I knew that the Hand of God was on you. If there was ever an immediate return on an investment, you are it. I pulled you up years ago and you have been pulling me up ever since.

To my editor, Marques Rice, thank you for your tireless work in editing my book. I could not think of a better person in the world to edit my first book. We have served together in ministry for nearly a decade. You have witnessed firsthand most of what I write about in this book. Thank you for being a friend, brother, co-laborer in ministry, and for helping make this dream a reality.

To my late Grandmother, Loretta Wheat, I wish you were here to hold this book. You would be so proud. You were my biggest cheerleader and my biggest fan. Every time I shared good news with you your face would light up and you would say, "Boy, God is using you." I love you and miss you so much. You would never let me leave your house without eating and in the same breath say, "Boy, you better watch your weight." The one piece of advice you gave that I will never forget was "Take care of yourself." This is so ironic coming from a lady who spent her life taking care of others. I love you Granny. I dedicate this book to you.

Table of Contents

Preface I

Introduction: Every church has a prayer responsibility 3

Chapter 1: Without Prayer, the Church Cannot… 11

Chapter 2: Take it to the Top 23

Chapter 3: The Making of a Prayer Leader 31

Chapter 4: The Necessary Qualities in a Prayer Leader 41

Chapter 5: A Price to Pray 53

Chapter 6: Five Pillars of a House of Prayer 59

Chapter 7: Seven Critical Targets for Prayer Leaders 73

Chapter 8: Things to Consider When Building a
              Prayer Department 83

Bonus: My Biggest Mistakes as a Prayer Leader 93

Reflections

Preface

This is a book about leading a prayer ministry in the House of the Lord. I wrote this book for those who have a burning passion to lead well and those who deeply desire to see their church become a house of prayer. You may not be ready for this book if you only have your toe in the proverbial pool. This book is for those who are committed to and cannot shake the call of prayer. I wrote this book just for you.

You are not just committed to prayer; you are a God-anointed prayer leader with a big heart! Maybe you are officially in a seat of leadership. Maybe you are an emerging leader. Or maybe you are a leader in seed form. You do not have the seat yet, but you have the anointing! As you read, you are going to feel like God is speaking *directly to you*.

Be aware of imposter syndrome as you go through the chapters of this book. Imposter syndrome will make you feel like you are faking this prayer leadership thing. There will be times when you do not feel ready. You may find yourself feeling embarrassed that you do not know more. Or you might think you should be further in your prayer life. Those thoughts will hold you back and eat at your core. There will be other times when what needs to happen does not happen fast enough. The enemy will attempt to frame it in a way that blames you.

Here is the reality: When you are doing everything you can there is no reason to question your own authenticity. Believe that and pour yourself into the call to lead prayer. Full commitment, full focus. You are an Innovative Prayer Leader.

Introduction:

Every church has a prayer responsibility

very church has a prayer responsibility. Those words were burned into my heart as I lay motionless on the floor after a powerful encounter with God. I will never forget the day; it was a late Sunday afternoon and one of my good friends, Dawn Cole, invited me and our mutual friend, Carlos, to visit a church. Dawn is a longtime friend of the family—like a sister to me—and one of the most solid Christians I know. Dawn is not the overly excited type; yet, on that Sunday afternoon, excited was the word. In fact, I cannot recall ever seeing Dawn so excited about something. She was emphatic about me seeing what was happening at this church and hearing the pastor preach.

Like most Sundays, I had already attended two services at my church and I was ready to go home, eat, and relax. Additionally, this church invite was on the other side of town in the opposite direction of my house. I was tired, hungry, and already dreading the drive home, but I had to see what Dawn was so excited about.

We arrived at the church about 45 minutes early to make sure we had a seat. The sanctuary was relatively small, holding no more than 150 people. And it was hot. I'm not talking about hot as in "good looking." I'm talking about a 90-degree-day-in-the-middle-of-a-humid-Chicago-summer hot, and this church had no air conditioning! But I thought to myself, "Well, I'm here now. I might as well enjoy the service." Plus, I wasn't worried about the devil showing up because it was too hot even for him. He was standing outside with a church fan in his hand praying that an ice cream truck would come. It was that hot.

The service starts and the worship team hits the ground running. The presence of God was so thick that, at one point, I felt like it lifted me off the ground. I literally looked down to make sure my feet were still on the floor. After the praise team finished, the pastor gets up and preaches. I will never forget the title of this life-changing sermon: Embracing Your Prophetic Responsibility. He preached from Numbers 11 and described how the spirit that was on Moses was put on the seventy elders and on the two men who were outside the camp and they prophesied. Every word hit me at my core.

After the sermon was over, I went down to the altar for prayer. The pastor ministered to and prayed for me. The only thing I remember after that is Dawn and Carlos helping me off the floor. We were the only ones left in the building and I knew something had changed. I already understood that everyone should pray, but, in that moment, God gave me stronger language to articulate His revelation on the topic: *Every church has a prayer responsibility*. More personally, God affirmed my assignment to be one of the people He uses to help people, families, and churches embrace their prayer responsibility.

Jesus reminded us of prayer's importance when He said, "My house shall be called a house of prayer." Although Jesus was speaking of a brick and mortar temple, Scripture also makes reference to other vessels being a house of prayer. Take a look at a few examples:

1. A person can be a house of prayer.

Do you not know that your body is a temple of the Holy Spirit who is within you, whom you have [received as a gift] from God, and that you are not your own [property]?
1 Corinthians 6:19 Amplified Bible

2. A family can be a house of prayer.

If it is unacceptable in your sight to serve the Lord, choose for yourselves this day whom you will serve: whether the gods which your fathers served that were on the other side of the River, or the gods of the Amorites in whose land you live; but as for me and my house, we will serve the Lord."
Joshua 24:15 Amplified Bible

3. A church can be a house of prayer.

So Peter was kept in prison, but fervent and persistent prayer for him was being made to God by the church.
Acts 12:5 Amplified Bible

4. A nation can be a house of prayer.

Then He said to me, "Son of man, these bones are the whole house of Israel. Behold, they say, 'Our bones are dried up and our hope is lost. We are completely cut off.'"
Ezekiel 37:11 Amplified Bible

Regardless of the type of vessel, Jesus said that every house has a prayer responsibility:

And Jesus entered the temple [grounds] and drove out [with force] all who were buying and selling [birds and animals for sacrifice] in the temple area, and He turned over the tables of the moneychangers [who made a profit exchanging foreign money for temple coinage] and the chairs of those who were selling doves [for sacrifice]. 13 Jesus said to them, "It is written [in Scripture], 'My house shall be called a house of prayer'; but you are making it a robbers' den."
Matthew 21:12 Amplified Bible

Jesus, full of grace and truth, walks into His house and sees it being used for unintended purposes. So, He sternly rid it of the religious practices that made it impossible to produce the power of God. If we keep reading Matthew 21, we see Jesus encounter a tree that failed to produce in accord with its intended purpose. Jesus curses the tree and it dies. The tree got no mercy. I pray that every person understands the risk here. The house deserved the same fate as the tree because it also failed to produce according to its intended purpose.

God does not play games when it comes to His house. In that scenario, God cleansed the house, but whenever God's people are disconnected for too long, we are in danger of being cut off. That is not popular in the times we live in, but, as my grandmother used to say, it's tight, but it's right.

Why was Jesus so preoccupied with prayer happening in the temple? As long as it was a house of prayer it was a house of power! When a church is not connected to God through prayer it becomes powerless. When prayer leaves, the Spirit and power of God leaves. When the spirit of God stops dealing with a person, a family, a church, or a nation, *that* spells trouble! Other spirits begin to invade that house and, before you know it, a place that was once a house of prayer is a den of thieves.

As you can see, the processes of cleansing, purging, and sanctifying are actually great displays of the Lord's mercy. They let us know that God still has plans for us. In Matthew 21, after Jesus cleansed the temple and restored it to a house of prayer, the power was restored and miracles, signs, and wonders returned! Check out verse 14.

And the blind and the lame came to Him in [the porticoes and courts of] the temple area, and He healed them.

Matthew 21:14 Amplified Bible

The encounter I had with God in that small church on a blazing hot Sunday afternoon is part of the reason you hold this book. You hold my promise to God to help people, families, churches, and nations become houses of prayer and display the plans God has for us. Child of God, it is His will and earnest desire that every church be a house of prayer. Every church! Every church that names the name of Jesus must embrace the work of prayer with open arms. The size of the church does not matter. The neighborhood, city, state, or country does not matter. The denomination does not matter. The pastor's economic status, political prowess, or popularity does not matter. It does not matter if you are led by an apostle, prophet, or evangelist. EVERY CHURCH HAS A PRAYER RESPONSIBILITY.

This book is a tool to show you how to do it. This book will walk you through every step of transforming your church into the House of Prayer that Jesus desires. By the end of this book you will be:

1. Better equipped to be a prayer leader in God's house

2. Better equipped to steward over the work of prayer in your church

3. Skilled at building or strengthening a powerful house of prayer

4. Prepared to strategically shift the culture of prayer in a church.

This book is a game changer for every leader and every church daring to go higher in prayer. Prayer is vitally important in pushing the vision and mission of your church. This book will transform churches, but what I love most is the process of transformation every prayer leader will experience as they go through this book. Who the prayer leader becomes in the process of building will be just as powerful as building the house of prayer itself.

Commit right now to finishing this book. Commit right now to doing the work. Commit right now to partnering with God and becoming the prayer leader that He created you to be.

Reflections

Reflections

Chapter 1:

Without Prayer, the Church Cannot…

There is a saying that "without prayer man cannot and without prayer God will not." It echoes Jesus' counsel in John 15 when He said "without Me you can do nothing." This holds true when examining the church's ability to fulfill its mission. In Mark 9, we encounter a demon-possessed boy. The boy's father approached Jesus' disciples and asked them to drive the spirit out of the boy. Surely, that would be an easy job for them. They were already casting out demons and this time it was only a boy. But they could not do it! The disciples quickly found out that there are certain assignments that require more than ministry as usual:

His disciples began asking Him privately, "Why were we unable to drive it out?" He replied to them, "This kind [of unclean spirit] cannot come out by anything but prayer [to the Father]."
Matthew 9:28-29 Amplified Bible

In other words, the church (disciples) could not fulfill its mission (removing a demon) because it was operating without prayer! Some of the most brilliantly gifted, creative, and talented people are in God's Kingdom. Yet, all the gifts, creativity, and talent in the world cannot replace what happens as a result of prayer. Without prayer, the church cannot fulfill its mission.

How does prayer help the church fulfill its mission?

There are two things that stand out to me when I reflect on my years of developing the skillset to help churches become houses of prayer. One, it has been wonderfully rewarding; two, it has been unexplainably difficult. I imagine this is what it is like to have a baby. Building a prayer ministry is spiritual work. It is faith work. It is also hard work. Be wary of anyone who says otherwise.

When prayer ministry gets hard (and it will), you must remember why it is important to continue the work: There are natural, spiritual, international, and generational implications connected to the church fulfilling its God-given missions. Prayer supports those missions. That is your *why*. Below, we will look at some specific ways that prayer supports the church's missions. Whenever you are ready to throw in the towel on building a prayer ministry, break this chapter open, re-read this list, remember your *why*, and get back in the game.

1. Prayer is the Will of God

It is the will of God that every church be a house of prayer:

Even those I will bring to My holy mountain and make them joyful in My house of prayer.

Their burnt offerings and their sacrifices will be acceptable on My altar; for My house will be called a house of prayer for all the peoples.
Isaiah 56:7

Scripture does not say God's house shall be called "the church with the most beautiful building" or "the church with the best creative arts team." Plain and simple, God wants the church to be a place where everyone goes to pray. That should be enough. The reality, though, is that that is not enough for most people.

Years ago, I surveyed one hundred pastors in the Chicagoland area and asked them to give me a list of five things a church must do. Prayer was unanimous. In fact, it was in the top three on every single list. Yet, the great majority of those pastors were not leading houses of prayer. Prayer was in their heads, but not in their hearts. Remind yourself that a praying church is the will of God!

2. Prayer Invites God into Our Activity

God wants to help us with everything. One of the greatest benefits of prayer is that it invites God, through the Holy Spirit, into our activities. Success in a church is often consistent with the prayers that are being prayed in that church.

As a member at my first church, we had an all-night prayer meeting where we were praying for members of our community. Our community was filled with crime, poverty, drugs, gangs, and prostitution. Yet, our church was on a mission to let everyone know that Jesus loved them and that God had a plan for their lives.

One of the people we prayed with that night was a man named David. David was a notorious gang member who had some major legal trouble. He did not want much to do with God, but we still asked God to help. The entire room wept and mourned and called out David's name in prayer for an hour.

On his court date, David prayed again. That criminal courtroom has probably logged more prayer time than any church in the community! David was facing more than twenty years in prison, but when the judge called David's case, no arresting officer stepped up. The judge ended up giving David two years of community service. And guess where he ended up performing that community service. Yes, at our church.

David is now a married pastor with two wonderful children; he was the best man in my wedding and he is in the last phase of getting his doctorate degree. What turned a notorious gang member into a loving family man and a pastor of a church? Prayer! We prayed and God helped. Look at what Jesus says in Matthew 7:

"Ask and keep on asking and it will be given to you; seek and keep on seeking and you will find; knock and keep on knocking and the door will be opened to you. For everyone who keeps on asking receives, and he who keeps on seeking finds, and to him who keeps on knocking, it will be opened. Or what man is there among you who, if his son asks for bread, will [instead] give him a stone? Or if he asks for a fish, will [instead] give him a snake? If you then, evil (sinful by nature) as you are, know how to give good and advantageous gifts to your children, how much more will your Father who is in heaven [perfect as He is] give what is good and advantageous to those who keep on asking Him."
Matthew 7:7-11 Amplified Bible

God can do things that the church could never do on its own, but you have to invite Him to the party if you want to see Him dance. A church that solicits God's help sets itself up to see Him do exceedingly and abundantly above what was asked or even thought possible.

3. Prayer Adds Power to the Preaching

In the late 1990s, I attended a Benny Hinn crusade in Chicago. I arrived at the event almost four hours early. I explained to one of the security people that I was a prayer leader in Chicago and I wanted to pray before the service. When I entered the arena, I was shocked to see that people were already there praying!

A woman who was praying told me that they always prayed before crusades, but it was what she said next that blew me away. She said that a number of people continued praying throughout the entire crusade. They were partnering their prayers with Benny Hinn's preaching. Suddenly, it made sense to me. The spiritual presence, healing, and deliverance during his crusades happened because there was a partnership between the preaching and the prayer.

We model this practice at my church. People are in prayer whenever someone gets up to preach the Word of God. Every time a minister gets up to preach the Word, there is a war happening in the unseen world. There is a war for souls to be saved, a war for people to be delivered, a war for the preacher to preach with boldness, and a war for an atmosphere conducive to God.

Preaching and prayer go hand in hand. Preaching was not intended to happen without prayer. History is filled with powerful examples of this partnership. Charles Finley, leader of the Second Great Awakening in the United States, attributes his success to his prayer partnership with Abel Clary. E4vangelist D. L Moody, founder of Moody Church and the Moody Bible Institute, had Marianne Adland as a prayer partner. Billy Graham, an evangelist who had 3.2 million people accept Christ under his ministry, had J. Edwin Orr as his prayer partner.

This partnership is also found in the Bible. Jesus prayed for Peter's faith before sending him to help build the early church (Luke 22:32). Epaphras prayed for the church in Colossae as it grew (Colossians 4:12). The apostles devoted themselves to the ministry of preaching and the ministry of prayer (Acts 6:4). Paul constantly asked the church to pray for him because he knew that his preaching was only as powerful as the prayers backing him (Ephesians 6:18-19; Colossians 4:3-4). The list goes on and on of the great things that God has done when preaching is accompanied by prayer.

4. Prayer Promotes Unity

One of the most profound prayers ever prayed is captured in some of Jesus' last words:

"I pray that they all may be one; just as You, Father, are in Me and I in You, that they also may be one in Us, so that the world may believe [without any doubt] that You sent Me."
John 17:21 Amplified Bible

If church unity could have happened without prayer Jesus would not have wasted some of His last, precious moments on the earth talking about it. A clear sign that a ministry is on the decline is when people cannot work together. If there is a lot of infighting and disagreement, if there is diminished joy, or if there is high turnover in the ranks of leaders and volunteers, there may be a disunity problem.

A couple years ago I was preaching at a church when the Lord revealed to me that there was a disunity problem. I reluctantly shared what the Lord showed me and instructed the church to have corporate prayer once a week for eight weeks. The pastor called me after that prayer period concluded. He said that his church had shifted! A few of the people who were causing problems had abruptly left the church and offerings had nearly doubled. Their corporate prayers led to unity.

5. Prayer Engages the Forces of Darkness

It is important to understand that we have an enemy. From the beginning of time, the devil's goal has been to separate mankind from God (Genesis 3). He accomplishes that task by stealing, killing, and destroying things designed to connect us to the Father (John 10:10). But we cannot resolve spiritual problems with carnal solutions. We engage the forces of spiritual darkness in prayer.

For our struggle is not against flesh and blood [contending only with physical opponents], but against the rulers, against the powers, against the world forces of this [present] darkness, against the spiritual forces of wickedness in the heavenly (supernatural) places.
Ephesians 6:12 Amplified Bible

Growing up in one of the toughest neighborhoods in Chicago taught me a lot about engaging evil. I realized at a very young age that you were going to lose if you did not fight back. Not only were you going to lose, but you were going to get beat up every single day. A church that does not fight back against the demonic forces that war for our children, families, and neighborhoods will end up losing children, families, and neighborhoods every day.

However, that weak mindset is not even in our spiritual DNA. Exodus 15:3 states, "the Lord is a warrior." Our God is a God of war! Engaging the forces of darkness through prayer is an important part of what we do. This is seen vividly in Daniel 10 when, in response to Daniel's prayers, God sent help from heaven to deal with the demonic forces that tried to impede His plan. This was true then and it's still true now. When a church prays, angels are released to help bring about the will of God.

6. Prayer Saves Time

What is the number one excuse people use for not praying consistently? Lack of time. What people fail to understand is that making time for prayer actually saves time.

At one successful church, the entire staff of about 70 people gathers for a weekly meeting. Everyone prays together for over an hour before the meeting starts. At one point, a consultant came in to conduct training and evaluations. The consultant eventually furnished a report to the pastor with one shocking recommendation: stop praying before weekly meetings. According to the consultant's calculations, the church was spending a lot of money on salaries and wasting precious time during prayer every week.

The pastor told the consultant that he respected his opinion, but he had already consulted Jesus about the prayer time. The pastor explained that most of the staff's greatest obstacles were overcome through prayer. He gave example after example of how prayer gave the wisdom and focus to avoid some very bad choices. Prayer was not wasting the church's time nor money; it was doing the exact opposite.

Jesus modeled this in His ministry. He went from one place to the next performing miracles. But He was always guided by what the Father revealed to Him. He did not waste time doing anything or staying anywhere that was not aligned with His revelations in prayer. In his message, "Prayer: Our Time-Saver," Dr. Stanley lists fourteen ways talking with God helps us become wise stewards of time:

Provides timely direction	Sharpens discernment
Prevents wrong decisions	Gives us energy
Eliminates worry and anxiety	Prevents distractions
Produces peacefulness	Reminds us to act now
Invites God into our activity	Protects us from discouragement
Produces confidence	Opens doors of opportunity
Eliminates fretting	Helps us discern between busyness and fruitfulness

Which of these benefits do you need the most? Spend less time wrestling with the hours in your day and make it your goal to pray first. You will see your priorities fall into place, feel your spirit relieved from the burden of diminishing time, and experience a peace that comes with spending every moment under the guidance of your heavenly Father.

7. Prayer Combats Pride and Promotes Humility

Some of the greatest battles waged by the church are chronicles of prideful infighting amongst volunteers, servants, and leaders. I could fill ten chapters discussing all the infighting I have heard about within the church (I am sure you have some good stories too). Pride is dangerous. I have seen people start humbly with God then get blessed and start walking in pride. I have seen entire churches walk in the spirit if pride.

Pride is dangerous because God opposes the proud. Pride puts us in direct opposition to God and opens a door to destruction (Proverbs 16:18). And make no mistake, a lack of humility is more than enough for God to halt His kingdom's benefits hitting the church:

Two men went up into the temple [enclosure] to pray, one a Pharisee and the other a tax collector. The Pharisee stood [ostentatiously] and began praying to himself [in a self-righteous way, saying]: 'God, I thank You that I am not like the rest of men—swindlers, unjust (dishonest), adulterers—or even like this tax collector. I fast twice a week; I pay tithes of all that I get.' But the tax collector, standing at a distance, would not even raise his eyes toward heaven, but was striking his chest [in humility and repentance], saying, 'God, be merciful and gracious to me, the [especially wicked] sinner [that I am]!' I tell you, this man went to his home justified [forgiven of the guilt of sin and placed in right standing with God] rather than the other man; for everyone who exalts himself will be humbled, but he who humbles himself [forsaking self-righteous pride] will be exalted.

I assure you and most solemnly say to you, whoever does not receive the kingdom of God [with faith and humility] like a child will not enter it at all.
Luke 18:9-14, 17 Amplified Bible

Pride has real consequences, but so does humility. God begins to perform miracles when the church leans into humility (2 Chronicles 7:14-15). God also gives grace to the humble (James 4:6). In truth, humility is the only appropriate response when we are in the presence of God's greatness (Isaiah 6:1-5). Look at what Paul prayed for the church of Colossae:

For this reason, since the day we heard about it, we have not stopped praying for you, asking [specifically] that you may be filled with the knowledge of His will in all spiritual wisdom [with insight into His purposes], and in understanding [of spiritual things], so that you will walk in a manner worthy of the Lord [displaying admirable character, moral courage, and personal integrity], to [fully] please Him in all things, bearing fruit in every good work and steadily growing in the knowledge of God [with deeper faith, clearer insight and fervent love for His precepts];
Colossians 1:9-10 Amplified Bible

Pride begins to diminish when a church leans into prayers like this. Praying that the church gains the knowledge of God's will helps overcome the temptation to place ourselves first. Praying that the church "display admirable character, moral courage, and personal integrity" combats infighting. These prayers put us in our proper place and brings God into focus.

Reflections

Reflections

Chapter 2:

Take it to the Top

I have heard it said that everything rises and falls with leadership. I agree. Leadership is essential to the success of any organization. We will deal with leadership, particularly in the area of prayer, in a later chapter. In this chapter, I would like to talk about the Leader of all Leaders: God Almighty. It is important to remember His position in the context of ministry.

Years ago I met with a young lady—let's call her Samantha—who had recently been placed over the prayer department at her local church. I was called in as a consultant to help her strengthen the pillar of prayer in her church. As we began conversing, to my surprise, tears formed in Samantha's eyes. She said, "Can I share something with you? Something I am afraid to tell my pastor?" I hesitated for a moment then said, "What is it?" "My pastor doesn't support the prayer department," Samantha responded.

Samantha went on to say the pastor did not attend any of the prayer meetings, he would not announce the prayer ministry's activities, and he had no idea what the ministry was doing. She felt helpless because church members viewed the pastor's behavior as a cue that prayer need not be taken seriously. Samantha was working hard, but she could not see how to improve the prayer ministry without support from the top.

I shared with Samantha that her pastor was not the top person at church; the top person at church was the pastor's wife. I was joking of course! I explained that there are two groups of people in church leadership: those who were sent by God and those who just went. If God leads you to the role, then He is always the top guy. If you take a role because you were asked by men, then someone else is the top person and maybe that *is* the pastor.

I asked Samantha if God told her to lead the prayer ministry. She nodded slowly, yes. That meant the help she needed was not from the pastor; she needed help from the Lord. "How long has it been since you went to the real top guy to ask for help? Have you taken this issue to Him?" This was still God's church and He was still on the throne. Samantha agreed that was the solution and she apologized for speaking badly about her pastor. I encouraged her and assured her that the pastor cared about the prayer ministry. After all, he paid for a consultant to come in to help. Samantha thanked me and vowed to take the issue to the top.

I have spoken with many prayer leaders who seemingly had this problem with their pastor. Ministry is hard enough just fighting our real enemy, the devil. Having unresolved conflict between key leaders, especially a prayer leader and a pastor, opens doors to all kinds of conflict throughout the ministry. As prayer leaders we must understand that problems must be taken to the top before they are taken anywhere else. God knows how to win His battles. Check out this passage in Chronicles 20:

He said, "Listen carefully, all [you people of] Judah, and you inhabitants of Jerusalem, and King Jehoshaphat. The Lord says this to you: 'Be not afraid or dismayed at this great multitude, for the battle is not yours, but God's. Go down against them tomorrow. Behold, they will come up by the ascent of Ziz, and you will find them at the end of the river valley, in front of the Wilderness of Jeruel. You need not fight in this battle; take your positions, stand and witness the salvation of the Lord who is with you, O Judah and Jerusalem. Do not fear or be dismayed; tomorrow go out against them, for the Lord is with you.'"
2 Chronicles 20:15-17 Amplified Bible

I did not want Samantha to discard the pastor's role in building a house of prayer. Pastors play a critical role, which we will discuss later on in this chapter. However, every now and then, prayer leaders need to be reminded of who the top guy really is. People who are successful in ministry understand what it means to take things to the top. There is wisdom at the top. There is knowledge at the top. There is peace at the top. There is joy at the top. There is favor at the top. God always knows what to do. As a praying leader, you must remember that God needs to stay involved in the process. Check out these scriptures showing that God desires to be involved and to help:

"The king's heart is like channels of water in the hand of the LORD; He turns it whichever way He wishes."
Proverbs 21:1 Amplified Bible

"I am the Vine; you are the branches. The one who remains in Me and I in him bears much fruit, for [otherwise] apart from Me [that is, cut off from vital union with Me] you can do nothing. If anyone does not remain in Me, he is thrown out like a [broken off] branch, and withers and dies; and they gather such branches and throw them into the fire, and they are burned. If you remain in Me and My words remain in you [that is, if we are vitally united and My message lives in your heart], ask whatever you wish and it will be done for you."
John 15:5-7 Amplified Bible

"Do not be anxious or worried about anything, but in everything [every circumstance and situation] by prayer and petition with thanksgiving, continue to make your [specific] requests known to God. And the peace of God [that peace which reassures the heart, that peace] which transcends all understanding, [that peace which] stands guard over your hearts and your minds in Christ Jesus [is yours]."
Philippians 4:6-7 Amplified Bible

Understanding the Role of a Senior Pastor in a House of Prayer

One of my late mentors used to say, "God gave the entire pie to the senior pastor, and the senior pastor can give someone none of the pie, a slice of the pie, or the entire pie." It took me some time to really appreciate the wisdom in that message, but, my God, do I appreciate it now. The senior pastor leads the church. They may decide to delegate a small or large portion of the stewardship in prayer. It is completely up to the pastor.

If a pastor is wise, he/she will make sure the work of prayer is properly and thoroughly stewarded. If youth ministries can have youth pastors and music ministries can have a minister of music, the church can and should make sure one of the most important ministries has dedicated stewardship. However, not every pastor will see the importance of prayer.

One pastor told me that prayer does not need oversight because people know prayer is right and they will always do it. I asked him if tithing and giving offerings were right. He said yes. I asked him if he would be willing to not take up tithes and offering for one month and just trust that people would give because they knew it was right. He immediately understood my point! Knowing what is right and doing what is right are two different things.

If you are called to pray, but you are at a church that does not value prayer you face one of two possibilities. The first is that God sent you there and He wants you to stay until His will is done in prayer. The second possibility is that you have to leave. You will never be able to pray enough to overcome the religious spirits that have overtaken that church. C. Peter Wagner, one of the greatest prayer teachers in modern history, said it this way, "The person has only two choices: stay where they are or go find another pastor; but, whatever they do, do it with honor."

The role of anyone called to assist a ministry in prayer is honor. We honor the men and women above us by supporting them in prayer. Check out these scriptures:

Remember your leaders [for it was they] who brought you the word of God; and consider the result of their conduct [the outcome of their godly lives], and imitate their faith [their conviction that God exists and is the Creator and Ruler of all things, the Provider of eternal salvation through Christ, and imitate their reliance on God with absolute trust and confidence in His power, wisdom, and goodness].
Hebrews 13:7 Amplified Bible

First of all, then, I urge that petitions (specific requests), prayers, intercessions (prayers for others) and thanksgivings be offered on behalf of all people, for kings and all who are in [positions of] high authority, so that we may live a peaceful and quiet life in all godliness and dignity. This [kind of praying] is good and acceptable and pleasing in the sight of God our Savior[.]
1 Timothy 2:1-3 Amplified Bible

When it comes to developing a prayer culture the church will only go as far as the pastor allows. As a prayer leader, you must get in the flow of the pastor's anointing and capacity because the anointing always flows from God to the pastor and then to the rest of the church.

It is like the precious oil [of consecration] poured on the head, Coming down on the beard, Even the beard of Aaron, Coming down upon the edge of his [priestly] robes [consecrating the whole body].
Psalm 133:2 Amplified Bible

In that sense, a culture of honor is the best approach. You may not always agree with the pastor, but you can always show honor. Anytime you have an issue with the earthly leader, always take it to the heavenly leader. See what the heavenly leader would have you to do concerning the earthly leader. This is a way to honor both and it keeps the flow of anointing in the ministry.

Reflections

Reflections

Chapter 3:

The Making of a Prayer Leader

Have you ever looked at your life and wished you were dealt a better hand? Have you ever thought that maybe, just maybe, you would be further along in life if the hand you were dealt was better? I have! Or maybe "why" was your word. Why were you born at a deficit? Why were you born into family dysfunction? Why did you have to experience a tragic loss? Why was it always hard to fit in? Why did you suffer with promiscuity? Why did you find the love of your life only for it to end in divorce? Why were you rejected? Why did you have to go through all of the hell you went through?

Or maybe the hand you were dealt was actually pretty good. You grew up in a loving and safe environment. Most of your childhood memories were good. You went to church and accepted Jesus relatively early in your life. Yet, internally there was a feeling that something is missing. Your outward battles were not hard, but the inward battles have been great! No matter the hand you were dealt, regardless of what you had to deal with or not deal with, your training had to be different. I want you to remember three things:

1. The devil desires to ascribe a meaning to your route that is not true.

2. The route was not sent to define you, but to remind you that all things are possible with God.

3. You are more prepared to lead your church in prayer than you think.

The devil desires to ascribe a meaning to your route that is not true.

I was having lunch with a pastor friend of mine when he said something that shocked me. He said he was looking at the events of his life and seriously questioning whether God had picked the right person. This pastor started to remind me of things he had done years ago (his past was in no way squeaky clean). The devil was using the man's past to chip away at his belief.

What began as unwavering, full belief that he was called to pastor was now only at the half mark. As a result, he half-believed God was going to use him to do great things. Half belief subconsciously caused him to only put half into his call. He was only doing half the work, attaching half of his heart to his commitments, maintaining half the focus, and living half the lifestyle. I let him talk for a few minutes and then I said, "That's the story where the *devil* is the author and finisher. That's the story without the Blood of Jesus."

Child of God, listen, there is another story; one that I like a lot better. It is the story where *God* is the author and the finisher. It is the story of your scarlet sins being whiter than snow. God has factored all of your shortcomings into His equation and, according to God's calculations, you are right on schedule. Maybe you wondered why your life or your route had to be so different. Please know that different is good. Your unique route—often sinful and sometimes painful—is one of the greatest gifts that God has ever given you.

In the early 2000s, I was one of the founding leaders in a ministry called the Sons of Thunder. During one of our corporate prayer meetings, I felt a sadness come upon me. I knew enough about prayer to understand that God had placed a prayer burden on me. A prayer burden is something that God wants to pray through us so that He can release a particular thing in the earth. I knew that I had to pray until the Holy Spirit removed the burden. Typically, the indication that a prayer burden has been removed is a strong sense of the joy of the Lord.

As I prayed and cried out to God, these words came out of my mouth: "Despise not your route." I had never heard that phrase a day in my life. I said it over and over again in prayer. *Despise not your route. Despise not your route. Despise not your route.* In other words, do not be angry with God about the route He chose to get you to your destination. That is really just a trick of the devil; he wants you to ascribe a false meaning to your journey. The route God chooses always brings glory to Himself through our lives.

Below is one of the clearest Biblical examples of despising one's route:

Now a certain man named Lazarus was sick. He was from Bethany, the village where Mary and her sister Martha lived. It was the Mary who anointed the Lord with perfume and wiped His feet with her hair, whose brother Lazarus was sick. So the sisters sent word to Him, saying, "Lord, he [our brother and Your friend] whom You love is sick." When Jesus heard this, He said, "This sickness will not end in death; but [on the contrary it is] for the glory and honor of God, so that the Son of God may be glorified by it." Now Jesus loved and was concerned about Martha and her sister and Lazarus [and considered them dear friends]. So [even] when He heard that Lazarus was sick, He stayed in the same place two more days.
John 11:1-8 Amplified Bible

When Lazarus eventually dies, Mary and Martha are devastated and confused. Look at what Martha, in verse 21, and Mary, in verse 32, say to Jesus:

"Lord, if You had been here, my brother would not have died."

They despised their painful route. To be fair to Mary and Martha, I doubt many of us would have handled this route very well. Their brother was sick and their friend, Jesus, had the power to heal. The route God chose would bring glory and honor to Him through Jesus. But the devil was trying to use the delay as proof that Jesus did not care about them. Many of you reading this book do not like the route that God used to get you to this point in your life. But God's plans always end in glory. Do not let the devil ascribe a meaning to your route that is not true. Do not despise your route.

The route was not sent to define you, but to remind you that all things are possible with God.

You are not what you went through. What God allowed you to go through should remind you that He is on your side! David was someone who did not let his route define him. David was not considered anything more than the kid brother who watched sheep. He was certainly not viewed as a warrior whom God would use to defeat a military weapon. David could have let his route—and the titles he assumed along that route—define him. But David knew he was not just a shepherd or a kid brother. More importantly, David understood that his route was littered with evidence that God could do anything.

Then Saul said to David, "You are not able to go against this Philistine to fight him. For you are [only] a young man and he has been a warrior since his youth." But David said to Saul, "Your servant was tending his father's sheep. When a lion or a bear came and took a lamb out of the flock, I went out after it and attacked it and rescued the lamb from its mouth; and when it rose up against me, I seized it by its whiskers and struck and killed it. Your servant has killed both the lion and the bear; and this uncircumcised Philistine will be like one of them, since he has taunted and defied the armies of the living God." David said, "The LORD who rescued me from the paw of the lion and from the paw of the bear, He will rescue me from the hand of this Philistine." And Saul said to David, "Go, and may the LORD be with you."
1 Samuel 17:33-37 Amplified Bible

What kind of God would allow a kid to fight a lion and a bear? The kind of God who wants to prove that anything is possible with His help. David, the little brother who watched sheep, learned to trust in God's power as he fought real dangers while alone.

You had seasons fighting things alone too. What have you gone through? What titles stuck to you because of that route? Drunk? Divorcee? Bankrupt? Forgotten? Abused? Neglected? Unintelligent? You are not what you went through! Do not accept that the activities connected to your route are titles describing who you are. God wants you to focus on your route as definitions of His power. God allowed certain things to happen along your route so He could prove that He is God.

See your route as David did. Focus on those private battles as proof that nothing is impossible with God. God has proven to you that He was with you the entire time. Your route was necessary. It was part of your training. The things you defeated in private have prepared you to publicly demonstrate God's greatness!

You are more prepared to lead your church in prayer than you think.

I may not know you personally and I may not know your name, but I know your type. I know the call of prayer is on you and you want to be used by God. I know you are ready to do whatever it takes to glorify God and complete the work of building a culture of prayer in the House of God.

But I also know that you feel that leading your church in prayer seems difficult and confusing. You are likely sitting in a seat that no one prepared for you. You probably have an amazing, encouraging pastor and other incredible leaders, but no one said to you, "I am going to show you how to be an Innovative Prayer Leader." No one equipped you for the kind of prayer ministry that you know your church needs. There was no passing of the torch; you are lucky if they gave you a handbook! And that is without mentioning the other challenges on your plate: spouse, kids, job, business, family, errands, and more. Cultivating your prayer life and dealing with life is no easy feat. You are looking for something or someone to help you make up ground quick, fast, and in a hurry.

Give yourself some grace!

You may not have all the answers, but you are more prepared to lead your church in prayer than you realize. I know because I was you. I traveled a similar path. For me, the prayer journey has centered on trying to accomplish four personal missions from God. First, call the body of Christ back to prayer. Second, teach people how to pray. Third, conduct prayer rallies and vigils throughout the world. Last, help local churches become houses of prayer. Seriously, God? Conducting prayer rallies and vigils throughout the world? I am from one of the poorest neighborhoods in Chicago! Well, yes, He was serious and you are now holding the book where I discuss the path of figuring things out - faking it until I made it.

My first attempt at leading a prayer ministry was in 1997. I was barely old enough to stay out past the time the street lights came on, but I was the head of a youth prayer ministry at the largest church in Chicago. Unfortunately, no one prepared me for the job. There was no manual on prayer, no handbook on prayer, no anything. I would have settled for some information written on a napkin! All I got was a position, a high five, and a hearty good luck. I wrote plan after plan, vision after vision, idea after idea, and tried one thing after another. About twelve years later, I realized that I had a trail of failures and a bunch of notes.

My next attempt at leading a prayer ministry happened when God told me to go to Pastor John Hannah's then-small church plant in Chicago. I grabbed my notes and promptly picked up where I left off: failing. By then, I realized that every failure leaves a clue for future success. Too bad no one told Pastor Hannah! I was stripped of the lead intercessor role.

My inability to figure things out began to bother me. I started to believe the lies that the devil was feeding me. *This is not going to work. They do not value you. They do not value prayer. They would do more to help you if they cared.*

Most prayer leaders I encounter have traveled this path. Just like me, you have endured it all. Just like me, you wanted to walk away, but you couldn't. Just like me, each problem or failure produced a clue. And just like me, all the clues you hold are about to come together to produce future success in leading a prayer ministry! Again, I know this because I am you. But more importantly, God knows:

"Before I formed you in the womb I knew you [and approved of you as My chosen instrument],

And before you were born I consecrated you [to Myself as My own]; I have appointed you as a prophet to the nations."
Jeremiah 1:5 Amplified Bible

Oh yes, you shaped me first inside, then out; you formed me in my mother's womb.

I thank you, High God—you're breathtaking! Body and soul, I am marvelously made! I worship in adoration—what a creation. You know me inside and out, you know every bone in my body;

You know exactly how I was made, bit by bit, how I was sculpted from nothing into something.

Like an open book, you watched me grow from conception to birth; all the stages of my life were spread out before you. The days of my life all prepared before I'd even lived one day.
Psalm 139:13-22 The Message Bible

Before you were born, God was at work! He already had you in mind. He formed you, knew you, approved you, set you apart, and anointed you. He knows you inside and out. He watched you grow. He was there at every stage. He knows about every failure and all of those happened *after* He selected you to one day lead a prayer ministry. God is going to use you to do great things in prayer. He knows that you are more prepared to lead than you think. Believe that with every fiber in your body and fully embrace the call to lead in prayer.

Reflections

Reflections

Chapter 4:

The Necessary Qualities in a Prayer Leader

Every major sport has a draft. A draft is the time that sports franchises add amateur players to improve their teams. Ken Griffey Jr., one of the greatest baseball players in modern time, was drafted first overall in his draft class. However, sports franchises do not always get it right. Two teams passed on selecting Michael Jordan, arguably the greatest basketball player to ever live. Tom Brady was drafted 199th. That means 198 other people were identified as being a better fit than the man who became the winningest quarterback in NFL history.

The process of trying to select the right person also plays out in prayer departments. When I first started consulting, I would often wonder about the process that went into selecting a prayer leader. Now, with 28 years of consulting experience, I have seen it all. In one of my first consultations, a pastor told me that he was going to make his eventual selection based on the following criteria: First, was the person a powerful intercessor? Second, how long had they served in ministry? And third, had the person given the pastor prophetic insight in the past? His criteria helped me understand why churches sometimes struggle to build a culture of prayer.

Just because a person is known as a powerful intercessor does not mean they know how to lead. Additionally, a person should not be selected to be a prayer leader because they have been at the church a long time. I think it is commendable to factor in longevity and loyalty, but that cannot outweigh a lack of leadership skills. Finally, prayer leaders should not be selected solely on their gift. A person can have a powerful gift and be a weak leader. I realized then that I had to create a tool to help pastors validly assess whether they were picking the right person to lead their prayer ministry. Here are the things that qualify someone to lead a prayer ministry in the local church:

1. Be a Person of Honor
2. Have the Heart of a Shepherd (Love People)
3. Lead by Example
4. Know How to Encourage
5. Have the Ability to Teach

Every pastor would do well by using this checklist to select a prayer leader. Every prayer leader would do well by cultivating these principles and skills.

Be a Person of Honor

Giving honor to God, who is the head of my life, to the Pastor, First Lady, and all the ministers in the house, I bring you greetings. If you have been around the African American church, any amount of time, you have likely heard someone get up and recite those words or something similar. If you have ever watched a court proceeding, you have likely heard the phrase, "All rise! This court is now in session. The Honorable Judge presiding." One of the Boy Scouts laws is "give honor to whom honor is due." But what is honor? How do you give honor?

Honor is dignity and respect ascribed to man or God. One of the most important attributes of a prayer leader is honor. Honoring man is a way to honor God; honoring God will cultivate a heart that desires to honor earthly leadership. I recommend that every person who desires to lead a prayer ministry do a thorough Bible study on the topic of honor. Biblical honor is a rather vast subject, so I will provide just a handful of ways to display honor as an Innovative Prayer Leader.

1. Honor with material possession

Tithing is the first expression of honor. It is an expression of trust in God and shows a level of spiritual maturity. It shows that a person is invested in their church.

Honor the Lord with your wealth. And with the first fruits of all your crops (income)[.]
Proverbs 3:9 Amplified Bible

Bring all the tithes (the tenth) into the storehouse, so that there may be food in My house, and test Me now in this," says the Lord of hosts, "if I will not open for you the windows of heaven and pour out for you [so great] a blessing until there is no more room to receive it.
Malachi 3:10 Amplified Bible

Every prayer leader in a church should give 10% of their income to the work of the church. I know this may seem like a given, but not all leaders tithe. If a person cannot honor God with their material possessions, it is an indication that they may struggle to honor their earthly leaders in other areas.

2. Honor through submission

Prayer leaders display honor by submitting to their pastor's vision for the church. That vision can include anything from the organizational structure of the church to the types of ministries in the house. Anytime I consult a church, I make sure the prayer leader understands the vision and I encourage them to help build what the pastor desires as it relates to the prayer ministry.

Let all things be done decently and in order.

1 Corinthians 14:40 King James Version

If the pastor puts a communication structure in place, honor it by following the protocols. If the prayer leader sees something that needs to be implemented, run it by the pastor. If the pastor says no, then show honor by not trying to underhandedly produce your own vision. One of the quickest ways to sink a prayer department or any other ministry is disorder. Disorder often leads to dishonor. A prayer leader who does not submit to a pastor will never be able to move their church into a culture of prayer.

3. Honor through prayer for the pastor

First of all, then, I urge that petitions (specific requests), prayers, intercessions (prayers for others) and thanksgivings be offered on behalf of all people, for kings and all who are in [positions of] high authority, so that we may live a peaceful and quiet life in all godliness and dignity.
1 Timothy 2:1-2 Amplified Bible

Praying for our leaders is a Biblical mandate, but there is a difference between praying and reciting empty words. I can usually spot when a person is not genuinely praying for their pastor. A telltale sign is if they speak negatively about the pastor. I am not saying a person has to agree with everything their pastor says or does. Neither am I saying that a person should bury their head in the sand and not speak out about evil acts or abuse. I am referring to a general, personal dislike for the pastor. It is impossible to bless a person with your prayers after cursing them with your words.

Have the Heart of a Shepherd (Love People)

I make it a point to visit other churches in my city a few times a year. One visit was memorable for a terrible reason. The beginning of service was what you would expect. People were pleasant, worship was good, and the Word of God was on point. It was what happened at the end of the service that shocked me.

I lingered for a while after the service was over. A few of the people who volunteered at the church were still in the sanctuary too. Out of nowhere, one of the leaders walks in, gathers all the volunteers, and begins to scream at the top of his lungs! He was pointing his finger at them and questioning their commitment to service. He told them if they missed the mark again, were out of place, or embarrassed him again there would be consequences! My jaw must have been on the ground. I couldn't believe my eyes or ears. I began to get angry, but I knew I was a visitor and I chose not to get in the middle of that situation.

That was the last time I visited that church. I wondered what would make a leader of the church think it was acceptable to talk to anyone like that, especially a group of volunteers. That leader did not have a shepherd's heart. He did not love those people. Innovative Prayer Leaders need a shepherd's heart to lead effectively. Leading, building, or overseeing the prayer work in church demands that you care about people.

Take care and be on guard for yourselves and for the whole flock over which the Holy Spirit has appointed you as overseers, to shepherd (tend, feed, guide) the church of God which He bought with His own blood.
Acts 20:28 Amplified Bible

"Then [in the final time] I will give you [spiritual] shepherds after My own heart, who will feed you with knowledge and [true] understanding.
Jeremiah 3:15 Amplified Bible

When it comes to being a prayer leader in church, in order to successfully sit in that seat, you must possess a love for the people you lead. This is especially important to the people serving under your authority because, ultimately, your character outweighs your title. If the character is not there, if the love for people is not there, then you are not ready to lead yet.

Lead by Example

My pastor, who is an exceptional leader, often says, "Leaders have to be above the people, with the people, and ahead of the people." In other words, they need to be detached from drama, have a heart connected to people's issues, and seek heavenly solutions. I agree. That is an example of true leadership. Leaders must lead by example. Nothing related to serving and prayer is beneath the prayer leader. Whatever the team is required to do, the leader should do. You also lead by example when you journey with the team through downtimes. It is easy to celebrate the victories, but you must be present for the struggles. That was a tough lesson I learned several years ago from a woman named Pastor Trimuel.

One afternoon, Pastor Trimuel and I were at Olive Garden having lunch. She looked me in the face and said, "If you do not stop running when things get hard you will never lay hold of the promise God has for you." She had observed that when things got tough for me, I would run from the team in the name of prayer. I used to think it was strong to hide my problems and deal with them alone in my prayer room. In reality, many times I would retreat and not even deal with the problem. She let me know that the time to lean into the team was when things got tough. Pastor Trimuel has gone on to be with the

Lord, but it is one of the most valuable things ever said to me and it will stay with me forever.

Know How to Encourage

If they only knew. Those were the words I said to myself as I rescued one of my intercessors from a rude church member. For the last several years our church has hosted an all-day prayer event called the Mid-Year Cry. Nearly 20,000 people attended our last event. We open the doors at the top of each hour and lock them ten minutes later. Whoever is not in the building when the doors close must wait until the top of the next hour.

We were in the ninth hour of prayer when someone told me someone was yelling at one of our intercessors. I rushed to see what was going on and discovered a church member who was upset because she was not allowed to enter after we locked the doors. This particular member was having no parts of the rules and she was saying terrible things about the intercessor. I knew this intercessor had just suffered a major loss and was facing difficult times. I knew she had been fasting and praying leading up to the event and had committed to serve several hours on-site. I also knew that she was rather new in the faith and still building confidence. So, after defusing the situation, I immediately focused on encouraging her.

As you can see from that story, serving in a prayer department can be a thankless ministry. Most of the work is done in private. And there is a difference between knowing you are needed and *feeling* you are needed. So, prayer leaders must possess the attribute of encouragement. Encouragement is a powerful retention tool. Servants are more likely to continue volunteering with joy when they can feel that same joy and love being poured into them.

I honestly believe that one of the major reasons intercessors drop out is because they are discouraged. That is why the prayer team at my church built an encouragement strategy into our organizational system. No intercessor can go M.I.A. without receiving a well-being call. We do this because sometimes people just need a little encouragement. Take a look at these scriptures:

not forsaking our meeting together [as believers for worship and instruction], as is the habit of some, but encouraging one another; and all the more [faithfully] as you see the day [of Christ's return] approaching.
Hebrews 10:25 Amplified Bible

Therefore encourage and comfort one another and build up one another, just as you are doing.
1 Thessalonians 5:11 Amplified Bible

Prayer leaders have to be intentional about encouraging those who serve on their teams. Celebrate them. Plan how you want to recognize them individually and collectively. Every prayer leader must be an encourager.

Have the Ability to Teach

People learn prayer in a number of ways, but I find these three to be most prevalent: Sometimes prayer is learned because it is sought, most times it is learned because it is caught, and other times prayer is learned because it is taught. We see all three is this passage:

It happened that while Jesus was praying in a certain place, after He finished, one of His disciples said to Him, "Lord, teach us to pray just as John also taught his disciples." He said to them, "When you pray, say: 'Father, hallowed be Your name. Your kingdom come. Give us each day our daily bread. And forgive us our sins, For we ourselves also forgive everyone who is indebted to us [who has offended or wronged us]. And lead us not into

temptation [but rescue us from evil].'"
Luke 11:1-4 Amplified Bible

Sought – The disciples went to the Jesus to learn how to pray

Caught – The disciples watched Jesus pray

Taught – Jesus told them how to pray

    The seat of leadership means that you are a teacher by default. Therefore, just like Jesus, a prayer leader must be able to teach people how to pray.

"My people are destroyed for lack of knowledge: because thou hast rejected knowledge, I will also reject thee, that thou shalt be no priest to me: seeing thou hast forgotten the law of thy God, I will also forget thy children."
Hosea 4:6 KJV

"Lest Satan should get an advantage of us: for we are not ignorant of his devices."
2 Corinthians 2:11 KJV

    At a minimum, a prayer leader should have a grasp of: (1) the definition of prayer, (2) the different kinds of prayer, (3) rules and laws that govern prayer, (4) the prayer teachings of Jesus, and (5) a disciplined life of prayer. Prayer leaders must be knowledgeable in each and be ready to teach.

Reflections

Reflections

Chapter 5:

A Price to Pray

The Currency for Spiritual Power

I grew up poor and without my father. By God's grace, a family in my community took a liking to me. The head of that family, Bernard Choice, told me that nothing in life was free. Most of the time he had two jobs and he went to work every day. Mr. Choice paid the price of hard work to care for his family.

In addition to modeling a serious work ethic for me, Mr. Choice took me to church. Although I found Jesus, I almost missed the kingdom! Mr. Choice's mantra that "nothing in life is free" did not line up with the pastor's message that salvation is free. On a serious note, salvation *is* free, but following God has a cost attached to it. It literally cost Jesus his life and it will cost you something too.

And He was saying to them all, "If anyone wishes to follow Me [as My disciple], he must deny himself [set aside selfish interests], and take up his cross daily [expressing a willingness to endure whatever may come] and follow Me [believing in Me, conforming to My example in living and, if need be, suffering or perhaps dying because of faith in Me].
Luke 9:23 Amplified Bible

There is a cost for following God's instruction. There is also a price to pay if you want an anointing to lead in prayer. More accurately, there is a price to *pray* for that anointing. The first time I ever heard that phrase was when David Yonggi Cho, founder of the largest church in the world, described how he was able to build that church. He said prayer and obedience was the "price to pray."

In order to be a man or woman of prayer, in order to lead a house of prayer, in order to be used by God in the vein of prayer, there is a hefty price to be prayed: You can *never* stop praying! We become whatever it is that we consistently do. So, if you want to lead a house of prayer, you must lead a consistent personal prayer life. There are no short cuts. There is no magic anointing line. There is no conference to attend. There are no books to read…even if the book is as good as this one. There may be times when you are tempted to not pray, but, remember, when there is no prayer, there is no power. There will always be a price to pray if you want to become a person of prayer.

Unless the Lord builds the house, They labor in vain who build it; Unless the Lord guards the city, the watchman keeps awake in vain.
Psalms 127:1 Amplified Bible

The hard work of building a culture and ministry of prayer requires prayer. There is no way around it. In fact, every successful Christian endeavor occurs because somebody prayed the price! You have to pray the price to get prayer into the hearts of men. You have to pray the price so God touches a leader. You have to pray the price to get the missing pieces on your team. Without prayer, any attempt to build in the Lord's House will be a fruitless attempt. You will suffer burnout, open a door for the enemy, and sow confusion.

Trust in and rely confidently on the Lord with all your heart. And do not rely on your own insight or understanding. In all your ways know and acknowledge and recognize Him, And He will make your paths straight and smooth [removing obstacles that block your way].
Proverbs 3:5-6 Amplified Bible

Prayer is not just reserved for the building phase; it is the ongoing catalyst for a powerful prayer ministry. Churches need five pillars in place if they are going to be strong in prayer (we will examine them in detail in the next chapter):

1. A leader responsible for prayer
2. An official prayer department overseeing prayer
3. Corporate prayer meetings
4. Teachings about prayer
5. A culture of prayer

Each one of those activities reinforces the others. Each one is an ongoing catalyst for more prayer! In the book of Colossians, Paul prayed that the church at Colossae would be fruitful [productive] in every good work. Obviously, prayer is one of the church's good works. So, amongst other things, Paul was praying that future efforts surrounding prayer would be productive. Each prayer department will look different depending on the size of the church; however, regardless of size, the price to pray and the ultimate goal is to be a church that never stops praying.

Reflections

Reflections

Chapter 6:

Five Pillars of a House of Prayer

It is easy to say that a church is a house of prayer, but how do you quantify it? What is the measuring stick for whether a church is actually a praying church? Chapter 5 introduced you to the five basic pillars of a house of prayer:

1. A leader responsible for prayer

2. An official prayer department overseeing prayer

3. Corporate prayer meetings

4. Teachings about prayer

5. A culture of prayer

Prayer Leader Pillar

In Chapters 3 and 4, we examined the traits and characteristics of an Innovative Prayer Leader, but all of that is meaningless if the church never creates the seat!

Ten years ago, my pastor decided that we should take prayer out of the four walls of the church and pray in the community. One of his dreams was to have a twenty-block prayer chain that stretched down 79th Street, one of the most dangerous streets in Chicago. We call it Prayer on the 9. In our first year, I was tasked with organizing the event and getting twenty churches in Chicagoland to participate. I was super excited about the opportunity and the first thing I did was reach out to every church in our zip code. But, to my surprise, only a very small percentage of those churches had prayer leaders.

I wanted to know if this was coincidence or the norm. After Prayer on the 9, I contacted one hundred churches to find out. It took a while, but I was determined. When I finally got to one hundred, I was saddened by the fact that only fifteen churches said they had a prayer leader. I asked myself then and I ask myself today, why is an area that is so important left without oversight? A house of prayer should have someone who is a steward over the work of prayer, right?

A quick word of caution here for pastors: do not rush out and drop someone in the seat just to say you have someone in the position. Make sure the person is ready.

"Don't appoint people to church leadership positions too hastily. If a person is involved in some serious sins, you don't want to become an unwitting accomplice."
1 Timothy 5:22 The Message Bible

Pastors, please avoid the pitfall of giving a leadership seat prematurely. The seat of the prayer leader is not for the faint at heart. Before giving authority, give responsibility. Watch people. Allow them to prove themselves as faithful before giving them a seat of authority. Taking away a task is much easier than removing someone from a seat of leadership.

There are a few things to consider when serving as the prayer leader. These are some of the lessons I have learned in my 20-plus years in that role:

1. Know your audience

Your audience helps determine the prayer strategy. The strategy you might use when leading a group of trained intercessors will be very different from the strategy you use when leading a congregation or the community. If the people in a prayer meeting appear lost it could mean you were leading at a level that left the audience behind. Always lead at a level *a little* above your audience.

2. Be prayed up

Spend time alone with God before you lead His people. Let Him deal with you. One of the worst places to go is a prayer meeting with a depressed, unorganized, or offended prayer leader. Be as healthy (spirit, soul, and body) as you possibly can when leading God's people. Grow, learn, and keep going after God in your personal life.

3. Plan! Plan! Plan!

The secret to prayer has been out of the bag for a very long time. Pray God's plan (1 John 5:13, 14). Prayerfully plan every time you lead a prayer meeting. Go into prayer meetings with His plan. Once you know what God wants to pray, you can work on tailoring it based on your audience. Sometimes God may edit the plan at the last minute. That is cool because it is *His* plan. Yet, that does not mean you should wait to get to the meeting to see what God is going to do. Plan, practice, and leave room for the Holy Spirit to edit.

4. Focus on God's Glory

To be totally transparent, I have often struggled with seeing higher value placed on things of less importance than prayer. Churches pay for music, children's ministries, administrators, marketing and media teams, lawyers, accountants, and so on. But when it comes to the prayer leader pillar, there is never anything in the budget. There is a pastor in Dayton, Ohio whose highest paid staff member is his prayer leader. I understand how outside of the box this is; in nearly half of the churches in America, the pastor does not take a salary. Many churches are not in a financial position to staff a prayer leader.

My point in bringing up the salary is that, even if your church can afford to budget for a prayer leader, you may never get a dime for your service and skills. True, many prayer leaders gladly do it for free. I have served as a prayer leader for over 20 years and I have never been offered a salary in that role at my church. But many people do not understand the level of work it takes to oversee this work. Or, worse, they simply do not value prayer. So, focus on doing everything for God's glory. I have discovered that He knows how to compensate everyone who works for him.

For every senior pastor, bishop, apostle, or other church leader reading this book, my prayer is that you would pray about staffing a prayer leader. Figure out how to obtain funding or a budget for your prayer leader. As you consider what it will take, think about the weight the prayer leader takes off of your shoulders both spiritually and naturally.

Prayer Department Pillar

Another pillar is having a department to oversee prayer. While everyone has a prayer responsibility, some people feel a special calling to prayer ministry. They have a burden for prayer and a mix of spiritual gifts that allows for efficiency in prayer. These people are called intercessors. Thomas Samuel identifies the identifying markers of an intercessor in his book, *Dynamics of Intercessory Prayer*:

1. Intercessors see and hear things through God's eyes

Seeing things through God's eyes is different than seeing the world with our natural eyes. We are able to pray with focus only when we see the world and its situations as God sees them (Nehemiah 1:1-5).

2. Intercessors are broken men and women of God

The things that break God's heart must break ours. Only then can true intercession begin. God's prophets were all broken men (Jeremiah 8:21).

3. Intercessors allow God to use them in prayer

Intercessors can become God's channels of blessing to others. Abraham was called of God not only to be blessed but also to be a blessing.

4. God takes note of Intercessors

Daniel was called "greatly beloved" by God, after he began interceding for his people (Daniel 10:11). An angel of the Lord put a mark on the foreheads of those who mourned for the land (Ezekiel 9:3-4).

No matter the size of a church, every church should have a prayer department. Although, you will not find the term "prayer department" written in scriptures, we do find the framework and principles for such a function in the Bible. As God raises up intercessors in a church, it would be wise for leadership to mobilize them by starting an Intercessory Prayer Department. Here are some of the key reasons churches need a prayer department:

1. Intercession and preaching go hand-in-hand (Colossians 1:9, Ephesians 1:17-18)

2. Intercessors function as modern day watchmen (Isaiah 62:6, 2 Samuel 18:24-27)

3. Prayer departments ensure that every church endeavor is covered in prayer (Deuteronomy 32:30)

4. Intercession is a ministry (1 Samuel 22:2)

5. Prayer departments help identify, mobilize, and utilize those called to intercession (Luke 2:36-38)

6. God seeks intercession (Ezekiel 22:30)

The prayer department is not the only factor that makes a church a house of prayer. Yet, as you can see from the list above, having a prayer department plays a very significant role.

Corporate Prayer Pillar

Call to Me and I will answer you and show you great and mighty things, fenced in and hidden, which you do not know (do not distinguish and recognize, have knowledge of and understand).
Jeremiah 33:3 Amplified Bible, Classic Edition

And when they heard that, they lifted up their voice to God with one accord, and said, Lord, thou art God, which hast made heaven, and earth, and the sea, and all that in them is:
Acts 4:24 King James Version

Chicago has some of the most schizophrenic weather in the entire world. The humidity in the summer will suffocate you, the subzero temperature in the winters will freeze you, and there are times when it feels like it rains for 40 days and 40 nights. And the worst thing about the weather is there are times when you get every season in the same day. You wake up and it is winter; by noon it is summer; by late afternoon there is a thunderstorm, and before the evening meal there is a blizzard. Even with all of that chaos, our church has never cancelled a corporate prayer meeting.

For over 11 years our church has had corporate prayer meetings at 4:00 a.m. on Tuesdays. One Tuesday morning—remember, 4:00 a.m.—the projected temperature was -20° F, with a wind chill that made it feel like -40° F. In case you are wondering, that is cold enough to instantly turn boiling water into snow! We did not cancel prayer. We moved to one of our smaller buildings in hopes that it would heat easier than a large sanctuary. We packed into the space because, even in a polar vortex, we needed to call upon God.

Nothing frightens the devil more than the people of God coming together to call on their Father for help. Corporate prayer says to God "we need help." It says to the devil, "Look, joker, we have help." There are many benefits to corporate prayer. There are also several things you need to consider. Let me give you a few of the benefits first:

1. It breaks the spirit of fear off a church

And now, Lord, observe their threats and grant to Your bond servants [full freedom] to declare Your message fearlessly[.]
Acts 4:29 Amplified Bible, Classic Edition

While most parents and guardians were busy trying to keep their kids out of trouble, my youth pastor was looking for the worst places in the country so he could send us to go minister. Someone told him about a documentary entitled *Banging in Little Rock* that highlighted the gang problem in Little Rock, Arkansas. After watching that documentary, my youth pastor knew that was our next mission trip.

You would be right to think that a group of church kids should be afraid to witness to a group of gang bangers in a dangerous community in another state. We were afraid at times. What moved us from fear to faith? It was the time we spent together in fasting and prayer. We never embarked upon a mission for God without God. We fasted and prayed until fear left and the boldness of the Lord came on each and every person.

2. It becomes the place of power

"Again I say to you, that if two [a]believers on earth agree [that is, are of one mind, in harmony] about anything that they ask [within the will of God], it will be done for them by My Father in heaven.
Matthew 18:19 Amplified Bible

One evening I was having a conversation with some of the founders and matriarchs of our, now, megachurch. They began to talk of the days when the church was just a vision in the heart of the pastor. They spoke of the times they prayed in agreement that God would do something great in and through our church. Today, everyone can see the fruit of those corporate prayers.

I believe that all great moves of God can be traced back to a people somewhere praying. The power of God is released in great ways when the people of God touch and agree in prayer. Corporate prayer is a force to be reckoned with because it generates power.

3. It releases a distinct sound

And when they had prayed, the place was shaken where they were assembled together; and they were all filled with the Holy Ghost, and they spake the word of God with boldness.
Acts 4:31 King James Version

And when THEY prayed

Shakened where THEY were assembled

And THEY were all filled

And THEY spake

Corporate prayer produces a sound like none other in the earth. When Robert's voice mixes with Suzanne's, when the elderly voices mix with the millennials,' when Caucasian voices mix with Latino voices, when the female voice mixes with the male, they all join together to produce a sound that shakes heaven and earth!

Once, when I was leading a corporate prayer meeting, I heard the spirit of God to tell me to pay attention. I looked around the room and noticed some people were praying out loud but others had their mouths closed. The spirit of the Lord instructed me to tell everyone to add to the sound. Then the Lord instructed me to "pay attention" a second time. The Holy Spirit said, "Notice the difference in the sound when everyone is praying." He explained that the sound in the room at that very moment could not be duplicated at any other time in history. Then I heard something that blew my mind. I heard the Lord say, "Corporate prayer leaves a voice print!"

A voice print is the mark that corporate prayer leaves on the church. Long after the meeting is over, there will be evidence that someone was there praying. Corporate prayer is the place when the people of God come together to release their distinct sound!

4. Corporate prayer reverses the plans of the enemy

So Peter was kept in prison, but fervent and persistent prayer for him was being made to God by the church.
Acts 12:5 Amplified Bible

The plans of the enemy can be reversed when a church comes together in corporate prayer! God has a desired outcome, man has a desired outcome, and the devil has a desired outcome. Prayer ensures that everyone gets on board with God's desired outcome! Peter was destined for death, but the Scripture tells us that the church prayed and he was saved. Prayer does not stop all bad things from happening, but it does give God a doorway to intervene if it be His will.

Teaching Prayer Pillar

Many people are forced to learn prayer through observation because their churches have no formal classes or systems in place to teach people how to pray. Sure, you can learn prayer through observation, but, as we know from reading about the disciples in Matthew 26, an opportunity to observe prayer is worthless if you keep falling asleep! Besides, learning through observation is limited. It is like trying to learn about an engine without lifting up the hood of the car. Yes, you hear the sound of the motor, but looking under the hood with a knowledgeable mechanic gives you a different perspective.

It happened that while Jesus was praying in a certain place, after He finished, one of His disciples said to Him, "Lord, teach us to pray just as John also taught his disciples."
Luke 11:1 Amplified Bible

This passage lets us know that both John the Baptist and Jesus taught various disciples how to pray. My pastor, John Hannah, often says we have to direct people to God. I agree! We have to direct people to God and one of the ways to do that is by teaching people to pray. I believe being taught, trained, and mentored is the most powerful way to learn prayer. Prayer should be taught from the pulpit, in classes, and through advanced workshops for intercessors and leaders in the church. A church cannot call itself a house of prayer if it does not teach prayer.

Prayer Culture Pillar

Culture develops out of shared behaviors and expectations. A childhood friend and I got saved around the same time but attended different churches. He joined a Pentecostal church and I joined a Baptist church. Although we serve the same God, our expressions in praise and worship differ. He does this fancy dancing and all I can do is clap and give the occasional toe tap. No one ever gave us lessons on the expression of praise; we simply conformed to the behaviors and expectations in our respective churches. Prayer is no different.

If your church does not have a culture of prayer, check the behaviors and expectations of church leadership. Look at whether the leaders talk about prayer *and* attend prayer. Pastors constantly ask me how our church gets thousands of people to attend our weekly prayer meetings and pack a building for prayer at 4:00 a.m. My answer is quite simple: People are simply following the leader. My pastor talks about prayer. He leads prayer. He regularly attends prayer meetings. We still have a packed house when the pastor is unable to attend because our church constantly highlight prayer's importance. Prayer is a part of our church's culture.

Also, when it comes to culture, I believe that percentages carry more power than actual numbers. Jesus views things by percentage:

And He sat down opposite the [temple] treasury, and began watching how the people were putting money into the [a]treasury. And many rich people were putting in large sums. A poor widow came and put in two small copper coins, which amount to a mite. Calling His disciples to Him, He said to them, "I assure you and most solemnly say to you, this poor widow put in [proportionally] more than all the contributors to the treasury. For they all contributed from their surplus, but she, from her poverty, put in all she had, all she had to live on."
Mark 12:41-44 Amplified Bible

A church with one thousand members and fifty intercessors (5%) is definitely not a house of prayer when compared to a church with fifty members and all fifty are intercessors (100%). So, it is not just about the pastor and leadership committing to prayer. The whole church has a prayer responsibility. It starts with leadership, but everyone has to buy in. That journey takes time and effort!

Speaking of effort, some churches may not be able to go to a location whenever they want to pray because they do not own a building. That just means putting in the effort to find a way to connect in prayer. As I write this book the world is facing a pandemic brought on by COVID-19 a.k.a. coronavirus. Almost every country in the world has ordered that people not be allowed outside for anything but essential services. All of the schools are closed. All of the movie theaters are closed. All of the malls are closed. And all of the church buildings are closed. How can the church be a house of prayer when there is no house to go to? Answer: virtual prayer rooms.

With today's technology there are zero reasons why the church cannot come together for prayer. Virtual prayer rooms are here to stay and I'm glad about it! Virtual prayer rooms can be just as powerful as regular prayer rooms, but it takes some work to make it happen. Let me walk you through a few important points related to virtual prayer rooms.

1. Limit distractions

In a virtual prayer room, just like in a regular prayer room, you want to make sure that distractions are limited. This includes background noise, pictures, uninvited guests, etc. The virtual prayer room should be considered Holy ground and treated with respect and a level of reverence.

2. Training

Whenever something is newly implemented, you want to train your people and have the procedures in writing. There are many seasoned prayer warriors who are not that keen on technology. Schedule a special training for all the people who are not familiar with the technology. This will go a long way towards making sure that no one feels left out.

3. Plan

Planning is the key to having success using virtual prayer rooms. Plan out every detail of the virtual prayer meeting to ensure it runs smoothly and people are able to pray effectively.

4. Pray

This may seem like something that goes without saying, but in my experience, when there is a lot of work or planning to do the prayer, output diminishes. Put prayer in the plan. Spend time in prayer covering the technology, people's ability to use the technology, and the feeling of connectedness that people experience even though prayer is happening in a virtual fashion.

Reflections

Reflections

Chapter 7:

Seven Critical Targets for Prayer Leaders

Key Targets for Successful Building

Through my years of praying the price to help churches become houses of prayer, seven critical prayer targets have always risen to the front of the line.

1. Pastor
2. Revelation
3. Assistance
4. Yourself
5. Endurance
6. Room
7. Souls

You may find others, but I have seen the results of strategically focusing on these targets. Let's take a brief look at each.

P - Pastor

Praying for your pastor is critical to building of a house of prayer. As an Innovative Prayer Leader, you must understand that the pastor plays a major role in crafting your church's prayer environment.

The church will only go as high as the pastor desires. Because of this, an Innovative Prayer Leader understands that it is important to pray over (1) the pastor's personal life and (2) the pastor's desire to see a thriving prayer ministry.

First of all, then, I admonish and urge that petitions, prayers, intercessions, and thanksgivings be offered on behalf of all men, For kings and all who are in positions of authority or high responsibility, that [outwardly] we may pass a quiet and undisturbed life [and inwardly] a peaceable one in all godliness and reverence and seriousness in every way.
1 Timothy 2:1-2 Amplified Bible

Let every person be loyally subject to the governing (civil) authorities. For there is no authority except God [by His permission, His sanction], and those that exist do so by God's appointment.
Romans 13:1 Amplified Bible

My pastor at New Life Covenant Southeast makes being the prayer leader easy. He is a man of prayer. He travels all around the world ministering the gospel and teaching on prayer. He loves prayer and he knows that it works. Yet, I pray for Pastor Hannah daily. I pray that his passion for prayer never burns out. As the pastor goes, so goes the church. Undergird your pastor in prayer. Pray that his/her passion for prayer never burns out.

R - Revelation

Throughout the process of building you will need revelation from heaven. Revelation is different from the systems and strategies we will discuss later in the book. The revelation I speak of deals with the spiritual insight needed to make the right move. One of the words translated as revelation in scripture is the word apokalupsis. It means disclosure, insight, to enlighten, and manifestation.

One of my most frequently used prayers comes from Colossians:

"For this reason, since the day we heard about it, we have not stopped praying for you, asking [specifically] that you may be filled with the knowledge of His will in all spiritual wisdom [with insight into His purposes], and in understanding [of spiritual things], so that you will walk in a manner worthy of the Lord [displaying admirable character, moral courage, and personal integrity], to [fully] please Him in all things, bearing fruit in every good work and steadily growing in the knowledge of God [with deeper faith, clearer insight and fervent love for His precepts];"
Colossians 1:9-10 Amplified Bible

Praying for revelation is important because spiritual things require spiritual insight. Spiritual insight allows you to build beyond what you see with your eyes. For example, God spoke to me through a dream where I saw a cyber-attack knock out the world's ability to use Wi-Fi for an extended period of time. I saw the church unable to use streaming and social media as a way to reach people.

My eyes currently see an uber-connected world; one that is difficult to picture without functioning internet. But the revelation I received through prayer about that dream led me to start preparing a prayer system that allows the church to function if that event becomes reality. It may seem far-fetched, but the world shutting down seemed far-fetched until the COVID-19 pandemic happened. No matter what hits you, your church, or the earth, heaven knows first. Make a habit out of asking God for revelation about what you are doing.

A - Assistance

Building a house of prayer takes more than a great strategy, great marketing, the right website, and the right social media platforms. Building for God requires two types of assistance: human assistance and angelic assistance. Let's look at a few scriptures discussing the human side:

Two are better than one because they have a more satisfying return for their labor; 10 for if [a]either of them falls, the one will lift up his companion. But

woe to him who is alone when he falls and does not have another to lift him up. Again, if two lie down together, then they keep warm; but how can one be warm alone? And though one can overpower him who is alone, two can resist him. A cord of three strands is not quickly broken.
Ecclesiastes 4: 9 - 12 Amplified Bible

I want you to think about how all this makes you more significant, not less. A body isn't just a single part blown up into something huge. It's all the different-but-similar parts arranged and functioning together. If Foot said, "I'm not elegant like Hand, embellished with rings; I guess I don't belong to this body," would that make it so? If Ear said, "I'm not beautiful like Eye, limpid and expressive; I don't deserve a place on the head," would you want to remove it from the body? If the body was all eye, how could it hear? If all ear, how could it smell? As it is, we see that God has carefully placed each part of the body right where he wanted it.
1 Corinthians 12:14-18 The Message Bible

      These two passages show the critical need for human assistance. You cannot build a house of prayer by yourself. You will need a team. The size of that team will vary based on the size of the ministry or the stage of the building process. In addition to human support, you need angelic team members. Angels are sent to assist the people of God in the affairs of God. Let's look at a few scriptures discussing the angelic side:

Are not all the angels ministering spirits sent out [by God] to serve (accompany, protect) those who will inherit salvation? [Of course they are!]
Hebrews 1:14 Amplified Bible

The angel of the Lord encamps around those who fear Him [with awe-inspired reverence and worship Him with obedience], And He rescues [each of] them.
Psalm 34:7 Amplified Bible

      Do not make a mistake and try to build a house of prayer on your own. Pray for your help on Earth and your help from heaven.

Y - Yourself

Do not forget to pray for yourself. You are responsible for you! I cannot tell you the number of leaders I encounter who forget to pray for themselves. This is especially true for those called to the ministry of prayer and intercession.

One of the first things I do whenever working with prayer mentees is administer an assessment of their prayer competencies. I assess their basic knowledge of the principles and laws of prayer. I look at their prayer habits and routines. I also look at what consumes most of their prayer time. I am always amazed to discover how little time they spend praying for their own natural and spiritual needs. Jude says it like this:

But you, beloved, build yourselves up on [the foundation of] your most holy faith [continually progress, rise like an edifice higher and higher], pray in the Holy Spirit,
Jude 1:20 Amplified Bible

One of the greatest blessings is to have someone to pray for you. But the responsibility to pray for you rests squarely on your own shoulders. How much time do you spend praying for you?

E - Endurance

Endurance is one of the most undervalued resources in building a house of prayer. I could write a whole book on that alone. I know its importance firsthand because I quit once. I was in my early days in ministry, I was a relatively new father, I had only been married for a few years, and I was experiencing pressure everywhere I turned. Life had gotten the best of me and I stopped going to church.

Don't judge me! I know I'm not the only one who wanted to quit or actually even quit. Every leader will be faced with reasons and opportunities to quit. Sometimes it is imposter syndrome, other times there is the feeling of being unappreciated. Sometimes it is the cares of life and sometimes it is the physical, emotional, or mental drain of leadership. How am I doing? Did you nod your head at all? I still experienced times I wanted to quit even after God miraculously delivered me. This is why I always pray for endurance. It takes stamina to build a house of prayer!

Therefore, my beloved brothers and sisters, be steadfast, immovable, always excelling in the work of the Lord [always doing your best and doing more than is needed], being continually aware that your labor [even to the point of exhaustion] in the Lord is not futile nor wasted [it is never without purpose].
1 Corinthians 15:58 Amplified Bible

R - Room

Ask God to make room for the prayer department in the church. When I speak of room I speak of two things: (1) a literal, physical room and (2) a spiritual space in the busyness/business of the church. This may seem like a small thing until you realize that prayer does not play a huge role in the functioning of most churches.

I have told many prayer leaders that foxes have holes and birds have nests, but prayer ministries have no place to do their praying. If you look at the artifacts of many churches, you will find that their founders had prayer in mind at the beginning. They wanted to make physical room and create spiritual space for prayer. Over time, though, the prayer rooms got turned into classrooms or storage. The spiritual space takes a back seat to things deemed to be more important. As God begins to stretch a church in the area of prayer, the church will have to make some critical choices based on room.

There was a time in my life where I served as an interim pastor of a church. An interim pastor is *very* different than a senior pastor. A senior pastor is the visionary shepherd, while the interim pastor is a stabilizing shepherd. As an interim pastor, I understood that stabilizing the church and moving the congregation forward could not happen without prayer. I talked to the board about my vision to implement some intentional times of prayer and they were all for it. The next question was a question of room. Is there room in the schedule? Is there room in the church building? Is there room for training? Is there room in the hearts of the key leaders to get on board?

The board agreed that prayer was important enough to make room. We found a physical space and we established a consistent prayer time for the entire congregation. Those corporate prayers worked; we experienced a shift! You could feel the joy of the Lord. The worship was more vibrant. People got saved. It all happened because we made room for prayer. In many cases, something has to go in order for prayer to come. Praying for that room—natural and spiritual—will be necessary to build a house of prayer.

S - Souls

Praying for souls to be saved keeps everything in perspective. There will be times when the work of prayer ministry becomes a very heavy burden. When those times occur, praying for souls will always bring you back to the reason you wanted to build a house of prayer in the first place.

This is not about the church's membership numbers. This is not about the number of followers one has on social media. This is not about who can build the best prayer department. This is not about monetization. This is all about winning souls for the Kingdom of God. This is about people being saved, delivered, and set free. This is about making disciples of men. This is about establishing God's Kingdom on earth. This is about people glorifying God by completing their life's work and dying in His will.

"For God so [greatly] loved and dearly prized the world, that He [even] gave His [One and] only begotten Son, so that whoever believes and trusts in Him [as Savior] shall not perish, but have eternal life. For God did not send the

Son into the world to judge and condemn the world [that is, to initiate the final judgment of the world], but that the world might be saved through Him. John 3:16-17 Amplified Bible

Jesus died for souls. Praying for souls has a way of putting that reality back into perspective. We can never get comfortable with people living life in the bondage of sin and then dying and going to hell. Innovative Prayer Leaders make praying for souls a priority.

Always remember that becoming a house of prayer *requires prayer*. Prayer must be the first step, the middle steps, and the final step. Prayer must be carried through each phase of the process and it should never stop. Are you ready to take the lead on these prayer targets and transform your church into a house of prayer?

Reflections

Reflections

Chapter 8:

Things to Consider When Building a Prayer Department

Transforming a church into a house of prayer is an exciting undertaking. But this is not just an exciting undertaking, it is a *huge* undertaking. If you are not strategic, the excitement can manifest as a tendency to want to do everything at once or become frustrated because things are not moving fast enough. Patience is a key part of this process. In reality, you want things to take time because you need to lay a good foundation. My spiritual mom used to say, "Lay a foundation big enough for what you want to build." Go through the process and build it the right way.

The standard operating procedures differ at each church, yet, I suggest completing the following steps when building a prayer department:

1. Get the Pastor's vision
2. Perform Assessments
3. Create a Purpose Statement
4. Create a Vision Statement
5. Create a Mission Statement
6. Create an Organizational System
7. Develop a Plan

8. Recruit

9. Develop a Prayer Strategy for the Team

10. Select a Launch/Relaunch Date

11. Create a Training Process

Step 1: Get the Pastor's Vision

The first step is understanding the pastor's vision for the prayer department. Do not overlook this step. When I consult churches on prayer, I always work with the pastor (or designated leader) for guidance on and approval of the plan. Sure, I know what it takes to build a culture of prayer, but producing what I desire is never the goal. The goal is for the pastor to write their vision for the prayer department and then discuss it for clarity. Below are some "pastor's vision" examples:

Example 1: My vision is to have a prayer department that prays for each service. I would like for the prayer department to handle the prayer requests that come into the church.

Example 2: My vision is to have a prayer department that undergirds the church 24/7.

Example 3: My vision is to have intercessors that can pray over every endeavor of this ministry.

Step 2: Perform Assessments

The pastor's vision tells you where you are headed. Assessments tell you where you are starting. Assessments are important because you cannot make changes until you fully understand what you are dealing with. The following questions are example topics to evaluate:

Assessment of the Church's Prayer Culture

Does the ministry have a prayer leader?

Does the ministry have a prayer department?

What artifacts point to prayer?

Does the ministry have a regular time of corporate prayer?

Is prayer training and development available in the ministry?

Does the church have a prayer room?

What are the stories of answered prayer within the ministry?

What are some active prayer initiatives?

What needs to be implemented?

Assessment of Things to Renovate, Eliminate, and Commemorate

What is broken that needs to be fixed to usher in a culture of prayer?

What is dead that needs to be buried to move beyond things that are religious relics?

What successes need to be immortalized and respected?

Once you have some answers to where you are and where you want to go, you can begin crafting foundational aspects of the prayer ministry like purpose, mission, and vision statements.

Step 3: Create a Purpose Statement

Every prayer ministry should have a purpose statement to keep everyone focused on the same vision. Your purpose statement should clearly articulate the reason the prayer department exists, *i.e.*, the Why. Try making the purpose statement something that is short and compelling, twenty-five words or less. Here is an example:

"The purpose of the [insert church name] Prayer Ministry is to train members on prayer strategy, develop leaders for corporate prayer, guide the body through intercession strategies, and intercede for the church leaders and members."

Step 4: Create a Vision Statement

The vision statement should be created based on the pastor's vision for the ministry. It should clearly articulate what you and church leadership consider to be the prayer department's identity. Again, aim for short and compelling. Here is an example:

"The vision of the Intercessory Prayer Department at New Life Covenant Church S.E. is to be a joyful prayer department reflecting Jesus, known for synergy, skillful intercessors, prayer warriors, highly organized teams, and a passion for the presence of God."

Step 5: Create a Mission Statement

The mission statement outlines future goals for the ministry. It should clearly articulate how the vision will be accomplished. Stick to twenty-five words or less. Here is an example:

"The mission for the prayer department is to conduct weekly in-person and conference call prayer meetings, implement quarterly prayer workshops, host annual prayer conferences, and train members as intercessory prayer leaders."

Step 6: Create an Organizational System

The organizational system details roles and responsibilities within the prayer department. This includes creating teams (1) assigned to pray over certain church ministries/functions and (2) that enhance the effectiveness of the prayer department, *e.g.*, workshop and training team, prayer conference team, communications/marketing team, etc.

Step 7: Develop a Plan

You develop a plan by pairing insights from the pastor's vision with answers to the assessment questions. The plan should highlight things you hope to accomplish at key points in time like launch, year one, year three, and five-plus years. The launch and first year plans are most important because they are focused on activities during times that will help establish the prayer ministry's effectiveness.

Launch plans will include things like the organizational structure, ideas to recruit members, and a marketing strategy. The marketing strategy should be based on research and data that shows what works best for the church's congregation. The launch plans might also include a ministry description, information about the target audience, and financial needs and responsibilities.

The first year plan is a cohesive, visual roadmap for the prayer ministry. It should include specific goals and objectives as well as a calendar with very detailed schedules of activities. You should also count the costs to get the prayer ministry up, running, and thriving. Look at all costs associated with events/meetings for the first 12 months and make a budget. You can use project management forms or one-year business plans as a model.

You should anticipate needing 30-45 days to draft all plans after completing steps 1 and 2. Submit the plans to the pastor for review. Make sure you give the pastor ample time to look over everything. The pastor may disapprove of certain items and require changes. Whatever the decision, you will need to schedule a meeting with the pastor to finalize the plan.

Depending on how your church is structured, the pastor may bring additional people in for plan approval. Pray together before the meeting. Ask God to consecrate your collective efforts surrounding this important ministry. And, of course, wait for final approval before doing anything else.

Step 8: Recruit

At this stage in the process, the prayer leader should recruit team members to help launch and run the ministry. You need to add the right people to your team. Recruitment strategies vary, but it is usually a good idea to focus on things that allow you to evaluate people, *e.g.*, servant fairs, new members' classes, workshops, conferences, webinars, etc.

Some people should be selected based on having skills necessary to complete the launch. Leaders should also select individuals who complement their skill set. I have found that people skilled in administration and those gifted to be helpers are extremely useful. Make sure to create intake and onboarding processes that are fast, organized, and user-friendly. You should also have a solid idea of how you will compile information about and communicate with your team. Are you going use a web database or a spreadsheet to track contact information? Are you going to communicate via e-mail, conference calls, or social media? Think these things through beforehand.

Step 9: Develop a Prayer Strategy for the Team

Your team needs to be connected through prayer. Prayer must always remain a priority. Develop a prayer strategy and timeline to pray with the team, *e.g.*, the first and third Wednesday evening each month from 7:00 p.m. – 7:30 p.m. This will help you stay aware of the spiritual and natural issues facing the people serving in the ministry.

"Without consultation and wise advice, plans are frustrated, But with many counselors they are established and succeed."
Proverbs 15:22 Amplified Bible

"...men who understood the times, with knowledge of what Israel should do..."
1 Chronicles 12:32 Amplified Bible

NEVER turn prayer time into a meeting time. One of the tricks of the devil is to make us believe that we can exchange our prayer time without consequence. In reality, he is stealing our prayer time!

"The thief comes only in order to steal and kill and destroy...."
John 10:10 Amplified Bible

We lose every time we exchange with the devil. Leaders, listen. When it is time to pray, it is time to pray! Make a commitment to your team's prayer time and keep it. Prayer is a whole success strategy! Do not neglect prayer!

Step 10: Set a Launch/Relaunch Date

The launch date is important because it not only provides an incentive to start the ministry work, but it will build promotional momentum for the ministry and market the vision. Research the best times to launch the new prayer ministry. Write all potential launch dates and list the pros and cons for each. Once voted on and approved, plan to launch (note: the date should be at least 3-6 months after the plan is approved).

The start of the prayer ministry should be an event. Plan to launch the prayer ministry by leveraging these tools: promotional materials, calendar of events, marketing and social media plan. Make sure you finalize all logistics for the coordination of ministry activities (plans that involve people, facilities, supplies, and overall costs).

Step 11: Create a Training Process

You need to train the people you recruited to the prayer ministry team. They need to understand their roles and expectations for those roles. What books or other resources should the ministry read? You also need to train the people who sign up to become members of the prayer ministry (intercessors). What will the intercessors be taught? Who will lead the training? When and how often will training take place? Be sure to include teaching on the ministry's core values (usually identified in the purpose, mission, and vision statements).

Reflections

Reflections

Bonus:

My Biggest Mistakes as a Prayer Leader

Most of this book is about what you need to do, say, and pray to establish yourself as an Innovative Prayer Leader; but your success also depends on avoiding certain pitfalls, traps, and landmines. A wise man learns from his mistakes. The wisest of men learn from the mistakes of *others*. In this section, I will share some of my biggest mistakes as a prayer leader. I invite you to learn from them. Before I share my list, I want to highlight a few honorable mentions:

Pitfall of Comparison: Keep your eyes on your work.

Pitfall of Pride: As gifted as you are, understand that the pastor is the leader.

Pitfall of Familiarity: Don't let relationship outweigh the need for professionalism and accountability.

Pitfall of Disappointment: Not everyone is cut out for the building stage.

Pitfall of Jesse: God will send many in seed form. Do not neglect to train them.

Avoid those pitfalls when you see them. Now, let's move on to the traps and landmines.

1. **Not taking counsel from my elders**

   The seasoned saints in my life have proven to be some of my biggest assets. But that was not always the case. My life as a young man, before I started ministry, was troubled. I did not have people showing me how to manage my life. And, because I was raised without much parental support, I did not find it easy to trust adults. That translated into me not trusting authority figures in any area of my life, including ministry. I looked to my peers whenever I needed help. I looked to my peers whenever I needed wisdom. I looked to my peers when I was building my team. And who do you think I selected when it was time to teach or lead prayer? Yes, my peers. This was a recipe for disaster that the Apostle Paul brought to our attention:

He must manage his own household well, keeping his children under control with all dignity [keeping them respectful and well-behaved] (for if a man does not know how to manage his own household, how will he take care of the church of God?). and He must not be a new convert, so that he will not [behave stupidly and] become conceited [by appointment to this high office] and fall into the [same] condemnation incurred by the devil [for his arrogance and pride].
1 Timothy 3:4-6 Amplified Bible

   The scars and the traumas of life will spill over into ministry if left unchecked. I had authority issues and I did not know how to handle life, but I was also arrogant because I had experienced some early success in ministry. I caused friction in the prayer department because I was alienating those who had gone before me.

   You should build upon what has already been established. Nurture a relationship with seasoned intercessors. Some of them may be younger than you in age but older than you in the faith. Recognize, acknowledge, and respect their wise counsel about your plans. Honor them and be sure to get their prayers. Always remember that you are on the same team, you have the same enemy and you have the same goals: see the church flourish, see people come to Christ, and please God.

2. **Being Married to the Position**

I remember owning my first car. I loved that vehicle! I paid for it in cash and it was mine. I viewed the prayer leader position the same way. I said it was my position, I prayed the price for it, I was in the seat, and I loved having it. But I learned a valuable lesson after being stripped of the position: Wear leadership loosely. There is a huge difference between owning responsibility and owning a position.

As an Innovative Prayer Leader you must understand that this is stewardship of the responsibility to lead prayer. An Innovative Prayer Leader never sees themselves *owning* the seat. Check out this passage. I think it shows the importance of wearing the leadership mantle loosely:

To one he gave five [a]talents, to another, two, and to another, one, each according to his own ability; and then he went on his journey. The one who had received the five talents went at once and traded with them, and he [made a profit and] gained five more. Likewise the one who had two [made a profit and] gained two more. But the one who had received the one went and dug a hole in the ground and hid his master's money. "Now after a long time the master of those servants returned and settled accounts with them. And the one who had received the five talents came and brought him five more, saying, 'Master, you entrusted to me five talents. See, I have [made a profit and] gained five more talents.' His master said to him, 'Well done, good and faithful servant. You have been faithful and trustworthy over a little, I will put you in charge of many things; share in the joy of your master.' "Also the one who had the two talents came forward, saying, 'Master, you entrusted two talents to me. See, I have [made a profit and] gained two more talents.' His master said to him, 'Well done, good and faithful servant. You have been faithful and trustworthy over a little, I will put you in charge of many things; share in the joy of your master.' "The one who had received one talent also came forward, saying, 'Master, I knew you to be a harsh and demanding man, reaping [the harvest] where you did not sow and gathering where you did not scatter seed. So I was afraid [to lose the talent], and I went and hid your talent in the ground. See, you have what is your own.' "But*

his master answered him, 'You wicked, lazy servant, you knew that I reap [the harvest] where I did not sow and gather where I did not scatter seed. Then you ought to have put my money with the bankers, and at my return I would have received my money back with interest. So take the talent away from him, and give it to the one who has the ten talents.'
Matthew 25:15-30 Amplified Bible

This passage gives a vivid illustration of the importance of stewardship. None of the servants in the text ever owned what was given to them. Their job was to wisely manage that which was given to them and produce a return. As an Innovative Prayer Leader your job is to produce, knowing that the seat of leadership does not belong to you. The pastor or other designated authority in the church can ask for the leadership seat at any time. Wear the leadership mantle loosely and wisely.

3. Ignoring Communication Problems

What do failed marriages have in common with failed ministries? Communication problems. Communication problems left unchecked will eat away at the prayer department like termites. You may not see it happening, you may not know it is happening, but, before you know it, everything that was built will come tumbling down.

Communication problems come in many different forms. Sometimes it is the people. Many leaders feel like they are great public speakers, so they are especially guilty of missing the fact that they may not be good communicators. Sometimes it is the system and not the people. If you know anything about the iPhone, you know that there are certain messages that cannot be delivered to an Android device. Regardless, poor communication steals production and is one of the fastest ways to lose your team.

And the Lord said, "Behold, they are one [unified] people, and they all have the same language. This is only the beginning of what they will do [in

rebellion against Me], and now no evil thing they imagine they can do will be impossible for them. Come, let Us (Father, Son, Holy Spirit) go down and there confuse and mix up their language, so that they will not understand one another's speech." So the Lord scattered them abroad from there over the surface of the entire earth; and they stopped building the city. Therefore the name of the city was [b]Babel—because there the Lord confused the language of the entire earth; and from that place the Lord scattered and dispersed them over the surface of all the earth.
Genesis 11:6-9 Amplified Bible

Poor communication causes division and a house divided against itself cannot stand (Mark 3:25). As an Innovative Prayer Leader, you must be willing to deal with communication problems in your organization head on. Communication problems do not fix themselves, they only get worse

4. **Not Clearly Defining Roles**

I grew up playing sports. One of the things I learned from sports is that everyone has a role to play. The coach has a role. The players have a role. The assistants have a role. When roles are not clear and people do not know what they should do the team typically loses. This is true whether you are talking about a sports team, a marriage, or a ministry.

One of the biggest mistakes I made in leading prayer ministry was failing to clearly define the various roles on my team. This caused confusion, wasted time, and I ended up losing two incredible team members. I was forced to expend a lot of energy fixing things that would not have needed fixing if the roles were clear. I have since vowed to never allow my team to go to battle and not know their role. As an Innovative Prayer Leader you must clearly define the role of every person on your team.

But all things must be done appropriately and in an orderly manner.
1 Corinthians 14:40 Amplified Bible

5. Not Chronicling the Journey

We do not talk about scribes much in our times. Yet, it is extremely important to chronicle the journey of building the house of prayer. It recently dawned on me that the majority of my leadership team had been with me for three years. This may not seem like a big thing, but when you take into account the warfare that goes with prayer ministry, the fact that we are all volunteers with very busy lives, and that we are building a prayer ministry in a big church, this is amazing. I am, however, missing parts of the story because I did not document all of it.

Every Innovative Prayer Leader should chronicle the highs and lows of the journey to becoming a house of prayer. We tend to remember the failures and forget the accomplishments. There will be things along the way that you will never forget; however, the small details are the things that will mean so much in the future. Writing the journey will help you see that God was right there the entire time.

6. Putting Great People in the Wrong Seat

How can a person be the greatest to ever play a sport and suck at a sport at the same time? Put them in the wrong sport. Michael Jordan is arguably the greatest basketball player to ever live. But there is *no* argument about his baseball career. He sucked. And the reason is clear: he was in the wrong sport.

I have made the mistake of putting great people in the wrong seat and it caused some of the biggest delays in building prayer ministry. I needed administrators, but I selected people who didn't have an administrative bone in their body. I needed pastoral people, but I selected people who struggled to love on people. It is not that those people were worthless; they were just meant to be great in other areas.

7. **Doing Too Much at One Time**

A few years ago I was doing training for a church and we were at the point in the program where people were able to ask questions. Someone asked me to give them one word that would be the glue to building prayer ministry. The word that came to mind was "patience."

"Consider it nothing but joy, my brothers and sisters, whenever you fall into various trials. Be assured that the testing of your faith [through experience] produces endurance [leading to spiritual maturity, and inner peace]. And let endurance have its perfect result and do a thorough work, so that you may be perfect and completely developed [in your faith], lacking in nothing."
James 1:2-4 Amplified Bible

Someone once said that patience is a virtue. As I look back at my time developing and building prayer ministries, I recognize moments that I wish I had been a bit more patient. When I first got into prayer ministry, I wanted to do everything at once. I wanted things to happen the second I thought of a good idea or the moment God showed me something new. That is not realistic or wise. Understand that you are bringing a team into the process with you. The line between boredom and breakdown can be thin. You never want to give your team so much work that they cannot be emotionally healthy and stable in their family life.